A VERY ASIAN GUIDE TO TAIWANESE FOOD

Written by **NANCY JENG**
Illustrated by **FELICIA LIANG**

WHAT IS TAIWANESE FOOD?

Taiwanese food is a celebration of fresh ingredients and rich flavors. Taiwan's tropical climate is home to many exotic fruits, earthy vegetables, and aromatic teas, many of which can only be found on the island. What makes Taiwanese food special is the playful blend of sweet and savory flavors and the humble nature of many of its dishes.

When European sailors first passed through Taiwan, they named it Formosa, or "beautiful island."

Many people live in big cities like Taipei, where getting street food is just as easy as cooking at home. Taiwan has a long culinary history, from its native cuisine to cultural influences from China, Japan, and Portugal. Today, Taiwan's culture is bigger than the island itself. Many popular Taiwanese snacks, drinks, and dishes are now enjoyed all over the world—you may have even tried some!

Scallion pancakes are a popular street food. Many vendors serve them from small carts, sometimes with a fried egg and sweet soy sauce.

SCALLION PANCAKE WITH FRIED EGG

SCALLION PANCAKE BURRITO

Modern cooks have made different versions of this dish, like scallion pancake burritos or scallion pancake pizzas.

SCALLION PANCAKE PIZZA

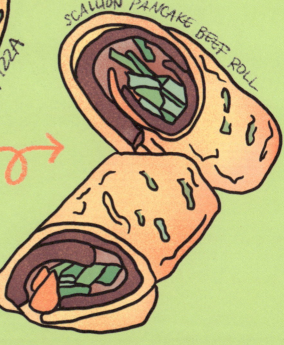

SCALLION PANCAKE BEEF ROLL

Another popular dish is a scallion pancake beef roll—tender beef with cucumbers, rolled up in a scallion pancake with hoisin sauce.

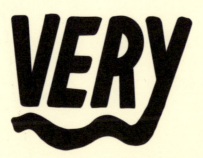

STINKY TOFU / 臭豆腐 (CHOH-DOH-FOO)

You'll smell it before you see it! Stinky tofu is one of the first things people try when they visit a night market. This is not your typical tofu—this tofu has been fermented and packs a pungent, aromatic smell. Those who are not put off by the scent will be rewarded with a delicious, savory treat, which happens to be the national snack of Taiwan!

It is usually served with a side of pickled cabbage.

Legend has it that stinky tofu was invented when a shop owner forgot about his supply of tofu and found it weeks later. After giving it a try, he was delighted to find that it was tasty and he started serving it to his customers.

STINKY

There are many ways to prepare stinky tofu—deep-fried, steamed, grilled, or stewed. The most popular style is deep-fried: crispy on the outside but chewy and soft on the inside.

You won't find this dish in many homes because it is quite stinky to make. It's best enjoyed with friends at the night market!

GUA BAO / 刈包 (GWAH-BAO)

Gua bao, also known as a pork belly bun, is a popular night market snack. Tender pork belly is served with powdered peanuts, pickled greens, and cilantro, sandwiched in a pillowy-soft folded bun.

This dish is also known as "tiger bites pig" because the bun is shaped like a tiger's mouth.

People often serve this in business settings, as it symbolizes wealth and prosperity (see how it's shaped like a wallet!).

TAIWANESE POPCORN CHICKEN / 鹽酥雞 (YEHN-SOO-JEE)

Taiwanese popcorn chicken is a treat for all ages—bite-sized pieces of chicken fried with delicious spices and served on the go. Many people enjoy it with boba milk tea.

This fried chicken is coated with sweet potato starch, which makes the texture super light and crispy.

VERY CRISPY

Served in a small paper bag with a long toothpick, this snack is easy to share and eat on the go.

VERY CONVENIENT

TEA EGGS / 茶葉蛋 (CHAH-YEH-DAHN)

One of the most common sights in Taiwan is tea eggs bobbing in a dark broth. Tea eggs are simmered in tea, soy sauce, and spices, making them a savory yet fragrant snack for a quick breakfast on the go!

Tea eggs are available at convenience stores all over Taiwan. When you walk in, you'll recognize the aromatic smell of simmering tea right away.

BEEF NOODLE SOUP / 牛肉麵
(NYOH-ROW-MYEN)

Beef noodle soup is so popular that it is considered one of the national dishes of Taiwan. Beef is cooked for many hours to create a rich broth that is poured over chewy long noodles.

Every year, a beef noodle festival is hosted in Taipei, where dozens of restaurants compete for the title of Best Beef Noodles.

VERy

There are many different types of noodles to choose from—thick or thin, machine made or handmade. Everyone has their own preference!

VERY COMFORTING

BRAISED PORK RICE BOWL / 滷肉飯 (LOO-ROW-FAHN)

Lu rou fan is a classic, home-cooked meal. Pork belly is slowly cooked with soy sauce, spices, and shiitake mushrooms and served with hard-boiled eggs. It is served over rice for a hearty and comforting meal.

The Taiwanese have a phrase "xia fan" (下飯), which describes dishes that go well with rice. Salty and flavorful dishes, like lu rou fan, go great with rice and make it even more enjoyable to eat.

VERY FILLING

Youtiao is a fried dough stick similar to a donut. Crunchy on the outside, it is often dipped in warm soy milk and eaten soft and soaked. Many people enjoy it sandwiched inside a piece of shao bing (sesame flatbread).

Fan tuan are stuffed sticky rice rolls. The center of the roll contains a youtiao along with other ingredients like egg or dried pork. It can be savory or sweet!

TAIWANESE BREAKFAST / 台灣早餐
(TAI-WAHN-DZOW-TSAN)

In the early morning, before the shops open and streets fill with people, locals gather at breakfast shops to start their day. Taiwanese breakfast includes a variety of satisfying breads and buns that always pair well with a warm bowl of sweet soy milk.

Put an egg on it! Other popular breakfast dishes include turnip cakes, baos, and scallion pancakes—usually with a fried egg added.

Peanut rice milk is another popular breakfast drink. It is creamy and has a smooth, nutty taste. It became popular because peanuts are often grown next to the plentiful rice fields.

ZONGZI / 粽子 (ZOHNG-ZUH)

Zongzi are pouches of steamed rice filled with braised pork, egg yolk, shiitake mushroom, peanuts, and chestnuts. They are wrapped tightly in bamboo leaves and folded into their recognizable pyramid-like shape.

Zongzi is as much family tradition as it is food. Every year, during the Dragon Boat Festival during late May or early June, family members gather to assemble zongzi together.

VERY GREEN

Sweet potato leaves: Once considered food for pigs, sweet potato leaves are now one of the most popular vegetables.

Taiwanese cabbage: Flatter and wider than regular cabbage, this variety has a sweeter, crisp taste that makes it a popular in stir-fries.

Taiwan bok choy: This variety is longer and leafier than regular bok choy. It holds up well in stir-fries and soups, keeping its crisp texture.

VEGETABLES / 青菜 (CHING-TSAI)

Eat your veggies! In Taiwan, children have many different types of vegetables to choose from. Taiwan is famous for its abundance of leafy green vegetables, which grow well in its tropical climate. Every meal has at least one stir-fried green vegetable. In fact, vegetables are so important that the word for "dish" (菜) is the same word as the word for "vegetable."

Water spinach: This vegetable is unique because it has a hollow stem. Its Chinese name translates to "open heart vegetable" (空心菜).

Water lily: This vegetable is the stem of a floating plant that can grow several feet long!

A-choy: Also known as Taiwanese lettuce, a-choy is crisp with tender leaves.

OYSTER OMELET / 蚵仔煎 (OH-AH-JIEN)

Oyster omelets are a popular and gooey street food, made with egg, oysters, and sweet potato starch, then covered in a sweet and sour sauce.

Oysters are a very common food in Taiwan, with oyster dishes often found near temples—a popular gathering place for people. Taiwan has many oyster farms in the marshlands along its southern coast.

Legend has it that the oyster omelet was invented by a general who, while trying to feed his starving army, found a bunch of oysters on the beach.

VERY GOOEY

Oyster omelets are commonly referred to by their Taiwanese Hokkien name, ô-á-chian. Taiwanese Hokkien is a language spoken natively by most of the population and is one of the national languages.

The key ingredient in oyster omelet is sweet potato starch, which gives it a chewy and gooey texture. Sweet potato starch is used widely in Taiwanese dishes because sweet potatoes are easy to grow on the island.

BOBA TEA / 珍珠奶茶 (ZHEN-ZHOO-NAI-CHAH)

Boba tea, pearl milk tea, bubble tea, tapioca milk tea—there are many names for this iconic and famous drink. It is a sweet drink made of tea, milk, sugar, and tapioca pearls (also called boba). It's fun to drink your boba with an extra-wide straw, big enough to suck up the tapioca pearls. Even though boba tea started in Taiwan, it's popular all over the world!

QQ, a word used to describe the texture of boba, is a modern twist on a Taiwanese Hokkien phrase, khiū, which describes food that is soft and bouncy when chewed. Boba is a great example of a QQ food!

FRUIT / 水果 (SHWAY-GWOH)

Taiwan is known by many as the Kingdom of Fruit. The island's tropical climate makes it a great place to grow almost any type of fruit you can imagine. Historically, Taiwan has been a large grower of pineapples, custard apples, bananas, dragon fruit, and guava. Many Taiwanese people enjoy their fruit sprinkled with plum powder or a sugar-ginger mix.

PINEAPPLE CAKE / 鳳梨酥 (FUHNG-LEE-SOO)

Pineapple cakes are one of the most well-known pastries and the most popular gift that people bring home as souvenirs from Taiwan. A jammy pineapple filling is surrounded by a buttery crust and baked in a small rectangular shape.

The word for pineapple, ong lai in Taiwanese Hokkien, also means the "arrival of luck." Many people give pineapple cakes to loved ones to wish them luck and fortune.

Taiwan is known for growing pineapples, which were brought to the island by the Portuguese in the 16th century.

SNOW ICE / 雪花冰 (SHREH-HWAH-BING)

This modern dessert is as fluffy as freshly fallen snow. Snow ice is especially popular during hot summer months. Unlike its cousin, shaved ice, snow ice is frozen, sweetened, flavored milk that is shaved into ultra-thin ribbons and covered with sauces and toppings.

Snow ice's texture is smooth and creamy compared to shaved ice, which tends to be crunchy. It's like a blend of shaved ice and ice cream!

You can top your snow ice with anything! Popular toppings include mango, red bean, sweetened condensed milk, pudding, mochi balls, ice cream, and fruit.

Aiyu jelly is a popular snow ice topping, but it is often served by itself with other toppings. This jelly is made from the seeds of a fig plant, which is native to Taiwan.

VERY AROMATIC

TEA / 茶 (CHAH)

Taiwan's climate produces some of the best teas in the world. In fact, people drink tea with almost every meal. Tea is such a big part of Taiwanese culture that it comes with its own pouring ceremony, art, and food pairings.

There are many mountainous regions in Taiwan with high elevation, cool air, and fertile soil that make it perfect for growing tea. The climate is especially ideal for growing oolong, one of the most popular teas in the world.

VERY ASIAN

Taiwanese food is a reflection of its creative and communal culture. While many dishes are deeply traditional, new interpretations and flavors are finding their way into homes and restaurants throughout the world.

Nai Nai's Scallion Pancake Recipe
蔥油餅 (TSOHNG-YOH-BING)

My nai nai (grandmother) used to make this scallion pancake all the time growing up. There was something calming about watching her chop the onions and roll the dough. As simple as this recipe is, it somehow always tasted a little different each time my nai nai, my mom, my sister, or I made it. We hope you can take this recipe and make it your own too.

Ingredients:
- ½ cup chopped scallions (green onions)
- 1 tsp sesame oil
- 2½ cups flour (and a little more for flouring the board)
- ½ tsp salt
- 1 cup hot water
- 1 tsp grapeseed, canola, or other cooking oil

Directions:
1. Mix the flour and hot water to form a soft dough. Shape it into a ball, cover with a damp cloth, and let it rest for 45 minutes.
2. On a floured surface, roll the dough out into a large circle. Drizzle it with the sesame oil and spread it evenly to cover the dough. Sprinkle it with the salt and green onions.
3. Roll the dough up into a long log and cut the log into quarters. You should now be able to see the spirals of green onions where you made your cuts.
4. Pinch and seal the ends so that the spirals and green onions are not showing. Lightly shape into balls and cover with a damp cloth to rest for another 30 minutes.
5. On a floured surface, roll out the four dough balls into a flat pancake shape. You can pan fry them immediately in a skillet or freeze them for later.
6. To pan-fry, add the cooking oil to a large flat pan. Cook on each side until browned, a few minutes each.

Papaya Milk Smoothie
木瓜牛奶 (MOO-GWAH-NYOH-NAI)

This sweet and refreshing drink barely needs a recipe—it's really a celebration of the delicious papaya fruit. While there are only a couple of ingredients, you can adjust the amounts to your taste: more papaya for a fruitier taste, more milk for a milkshake consistency, whole ice cubes for a colder, thicker smoothie, or just enough shaved ice to make it cold. In some places, the papaya is so sweet that no sugar is needed at all.

Ingredients:
- ½ of a medium-sized papaya
- ½ cup milk
- 1 cup of ice cubes (more if you prefer it thicker)
- 1 tbsp sugar, adjusted to taste

Directions:
1. Cut a papaya in half and remove the seeds. Peel and cut into large chunks.
2. Put the papaya, milk, and ice into a blender. Blend until smooth.
3. Taste and add sugar as needed.

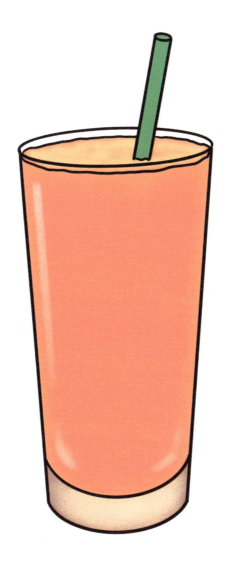

Tea Eggs
茶葉蛋 (CHAH-YEH-DAHN)

Tea eggs can be made a variety of ways with different teas and spices. No matter the ingredients, you can count on tea eggs to be an aromatic, easy snack with a beautiful marbled appearance.

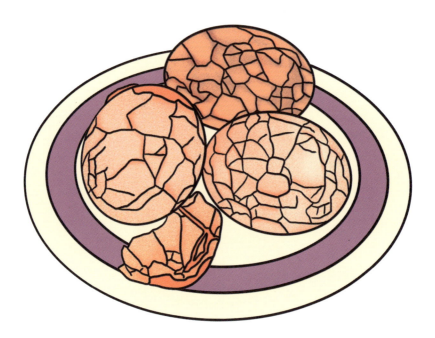

Ingredients:
- 6 eggs
- 2 star anise
- ¼ cup soy sauce
- 2 tbsp black tea leaves
- 1 cinnamon stick

Directions:
1. Put all the ingredients in a pot and cover with water.
2. Bring to a boil, then simmer for 10 minutes.
3. While the eggs are boiling, prepare an ice bath. After ten minutes remove the eggs from the pot and place them in an ice bath to cool them down.
4. Use a spoon or your kitchen counter to tap the eggs and create cracks in the shell.
5. Put the eggs back into the liquid and let it steep overnight or for about 12 hours. After that, they'll be ready to eat!

In loving memory of Nai Nai, forever queen of the kitchen. To Ray, Terry, Susan, and Brett, forever my eating companions. –N.J.

To A-Ma, Mom, Dad, Isaac, Kevin, my Taiwanese-American friends and community I've met around the world, and everyone who has supported my artist journey thus far. –F.L.

A Very Asian Guide to Taiwanese Food is first published by Gloo Books 2025.
Written by Nancy Jeng.
Illustrated by Felicia Liang.
The illustrations in this book were rendered in a digital medium.
Text copyright © 2025 Nancy Jeng
Illustrations copyright © 2025 Gloo Books

All rights reserved. No part of this book may be reproduced in any form or used in any manner without permission from the publisher, except for use of brief quotations in reviews or other noncommercial uses permitted by copyright law.

For more information or to order books, please visit www.gloobooks.com or contact us at contact@gloobooks.com. Follow us at @gloobooks.

ISBN: 978-1-962351-23-2

Printed in Korea.